Skira Architecture Library

West 8

Skira

Editor
Luca Molinari

Editing
Anna Albano

Layout
Paola Ranzini

First published in Italy in 2000 by
Skira editore S.p.A.
Palazzo Casati Stampa
via Torino 61
20123 Milano
Italy

Printed and bound in Italy. First edition

ISBN 88-8118-655-1

Distributed in North America and Latin
America by Abbeville Publishing Group,
22 Cortlandt Street, New York,
NY 10007, USA.
Distributed elsewhere in the world by
Thames and Hudson Ltd., 181a High
Holborn, London WC1V 7QX,
United Kingdom.

Contents

9   Introduction
Adriaan Geuze

14   How much is one million?
16   Wildlife
18   Zeppelin
base
24   Borneo Sporenburg - 2500 Voids
42   Ypenburg
colonisation
50   Buckthorn City
54   Riem Park - Virgin city
58   Zeeburg Island
60   Vertical Landscape
void
68   ABN Amro Bank
72   Theatre Square
84   Kremlin
88   Cemetery San Michele
totem
98   Leidsche Rijn Bridges
104   Borneo Sporenburg Bridges
114   Elevated walkway
120   Carrasco Square
126   Aegon Square
130   Expo-02 - Landscape versus media
contemplation
142   Secret Garden
146   Nymph Garden
150   Cypresses Garden
159   Project credits

After twelve years West 8 continues on the undefinable field of urban design, architecture, public space and landscape and product design. Innovating and exploring by ignoring the unwritten laws of traditional design attitudes, by crossing the boundaries of these professional fields. This Skira publication somehow reflects the crossover research of West 8. In five chapters specific positions in the contemporary city are elaborated: base, colonisation, void, totem, contemplation.

Special thanks to the editor Luca Molinari.

Rotterdam, May 2000

Adriaan Geuze

Introduction

Diagnose

The contemporary landscape is a collage of different territories cut up by athletic infrastructures. Rural landscape, nature and city archaeology of century's extensions form an amalgam. Unhindered by architectonic doctrine or morality, the city approaches the horizon or shoots into the sky. The existing metropolitan landscape shows the fabulous scenery, which goes beyond the dreams of the avant-garde and pre-war surrealist. The periphery and the expanding suburban planes absorb large-scale facilities, urban subcentres and industrial complexes. The city creates it's own new wastelands and isolated fragments. The 24-hours-clock and motion is the new soul of this landscape. The contemporary citizen enjoys his urban landscape and changes his position every hour, everyday, every week; has many telephone numbers and addresses.

By driving a car or catching the subway the image of the city is a scenic sequence static with signs and objects passing by. The periphery has a morphology with a charming beauty different from the traditional city but not necessarily less attractive. The urban sprawl is the mirror of the mass culture. It has hypnotising qualities but also lacks authenticity. Contemporary landscape escapes the traditional urban ideas because no model suits its banal reality.

Understanding the contemporary life and society, architectonic design anchors and statements for urban planning should be redefined.

Within the recent work of West 8 a few specific conditions are explored which directly link to an optimistic recognition of this contemporary city.

Base
A contemporary citizen with his mobile lifestyle and ever changing addresses and activities should not be pushed to live in a functionalist home with a 'view' over Arcadian nature; the modernist ideal.

The classic city-neighbourhood of blocks and streets is not for the contemporary, who desires just a base. A unit from which he organises his life and from where he jumps into the world, works, travels and gathers social contacts. This base should not necessarily be a 'complete house' with a living, bedroom, kitchen, balcony, garage and garden with fence. It could be less complex and less developed than this 'house'. There is no individual universe or a unique home anymore. There is no more vital or harmonious nature to elevate the Corbusian apartment blocks. The individual has no desire to celebrate the cliché view offered by the modernists window on a lifeless romantic urban environment. A large barn, a patio with high studio, a tower with small rooms: anything can be used as a base. From this container he adds the beach, a family house in the countryside, mum's coffeetable, a hotel roof for the weekly work, a sushi-kitchen, a bath shared with a friend, etc.

Is it possible to use this base as a key element for urban planning? What does it look like? In which configuration will it be organised? The possible definition could be related to a few conditions of contemporary mass society.

First, the base is an address, to be connected with the infrastructural networks, both mass media and physical transport systems. It welcomes the car, the bypass and the freeway culture. The base should be designed as a drive-in, a drive-on, a drive-over. The convenience of the car and the beauty of car design are an elementary inspiration for it's design.

Second, the need for individuality, intimacy, and privacy. In the hectic contemporary life with hundreds of decisions and fragmented landscapes, it should be a safe and defined spot that prioritises enclosure before the view. The base is probably introverted and incorporates nature within instead of exposure to it.

The third potential character of the base is its undefined floor plan. Everybody demands a specific home, adaptable for different characters. One for the girl with two Harley bikes and no kids, another will be the focal point in the life of a single parent lawyer with three recalcitrant adolescents or the mountaineer with steep staircases.

Forth, is the entrance, the gate to the hectic life. The architecture is not a complicated composition but expresses simplicity and clarity and tries to catch the daylight without losing privacy.

The architecture of the base is the opposite from the modernist optimum of floor plan based on standardised sizes, surfaces and the hysteric celebration of the window view. From its interior the view on the city or the landscape is more indirect and unattended. Like in the magic paintings by Vermeer, the window still exists, not showing an image, but offering a strong presence of the outside world. Architecture becomes an art of composing spaces, catching daylight, integrating outside void and hiding from the chaotic urban environment.

Like a caveman, hunting and collecting for weeks in a chaotic and violent nature, finally returning to feed the tribe, to fertilise the women and to be hypnotised in ritual dance around the fire, the contemporary city-dweller always returns to base.

Colonisation

How to position new urban settlements in a contemporary landscape lacking any specific identity? One of the strongest desires to locate a potential new settlement would be a virgin nature, a meandering river or a coastline with tabletop mountains. These conditions exist only as preserved landscape, like wilderness reserves and other environmental taboos.

Instead of reprinting traditional urban tissue without any authentic environmental context, urban planners better create new man-made nature: regenerated forests, landfills and agricultural plantations, new landscape to be colonised. This new wilderness should not be freed from human activity but should manifest characteristics to be used for new occupation by the next generation. Abandoned industrial sites, forgotten airstrips and brownfields can be transformed in new nature.

Void Totem Contemplation

One negative aspect of the landscape of the mass-culture is the lack of non-defined space. To accommodate mass-culture, the contemporary city is organised into one-dimensional space and experience. Every single part is designed for one function only. It manifests monoculture. The city-dweller is mobile and exchanging cultures: consuming like in a supermarket shopper. The euphoria of the mass-culture principally creates a numb individual. Efficiency, defined regulations and even law prevent the urban dweller from interpreting the environment in his own way. In modern functionalist urban planning every site, every spot has a given specific meaning. To exist, a human being must be able to take in the environment in his own way.

Amidst the urban landscape, introvert spaces and illusive ob-

jects play an important role. The organised world of commerce, with its functionality and efficiency, finds its inevitable counterpart in specific spaces that appeal to doubt, mortality, desire and perversity. The straight jacket of culture for the masses makes the city dweller crave for platforms inviting exhibitionism, apocalyptic sensations and the beauty of silence.
The hunting instinct of the Homo sapiens still exists in the contemporary city-dweller and his capacity to identify with the landscape is continuously evolving. The contemporary city-dweller is self-assured and intelligent. He has the capacity to anticipate changes in his environment and adapt like a chameleon. The daily trips from work, to home, to school, to sports facilities or to friends and family are ritual journeys through challenging surroundings.

On these trips signs and symbols guide the route. In the classic city, life is captured in a static hierarchy. The modernist city produces an efficient layout of urban programme and circulation. Contemporary urban planning should create non-identifiable objects, secret gardens, and voids. The urban hiker is challenged by elements and spaces of unpredictable presence; tribute to creativity, able to fly.

How much is one million?

Quantitative research
In Holland stands a house
Scale model of 800,000 houses
Exhibit: Netherlands Architecture
Institute, 1995

Since 1995 city planning in the Netherlands has called for the production of over 100 thousand homes per year. Most of this new housing has been developed in suburban environments. In the sixties, as the period of post-war reconstruction ended, it appeared that rural pastures were slowly but surely becoming densely developed with family housing. The first million new homes were built between World War II through the sixties. The government's decision to realise another one million homes before 2005 was made tangible is a scale-model of 800 thousand identical houses. The overwhelming sea of housing challenged onlookers to consider and form opinions on planning and zoning on this scale.

Wildlife

Study on density
Study AIR, Alexanderpolder
Commissioner: Rotterdamse
Kunststichting, 1993

Creeping suburban sprawl is examined in a study of the potential densities and quantities that could be reached in the Netherlands. The urban agglomeration of Western Holland includes an area of 175,000 'empty' hectare, which may not be developed. This so-called Green Heart between Amsterdam, The Hague, Rotterdam and Utrecht has been declared a no-go zone for any sort of development. Nevertheless, the adjacent municipalities are nibbling away at the boundaries, and sooner or later the Green Heart will be consumed stealthily unless a plan of action is adopted. Based on the actual demand for housing in the Alexanderpolder, close by Rotterdam, various scenarios for developing the Green Heart were explored. The plan for the Alexanderpolder area contains a mixture of differing densities. Its flexibility contrasts sharply with homogenous new estate developments that, in an effort to spare the landscape, are compact and introverted, but fail to fit in either with the landscape or with neighbouring cities.

Zeppelin

Morphological analysis of the suburban city
Video stills from 'Colonising the void'
(two tapes)
VI Mostra Internazionale di Architettura,
Venice, 1996
Commissioner: Kristin Feireiss, Netherlands
Architecture Institute, Kunstkanaal (video).

Viewed from the air, the dramatic scale of Dutch suburban cities becomes visible. The abstract patterns of sub-divided pastures and residential areas alternate like exchangeable pieces in an endless puzzle. The video camera registers undeveloped green parcels, where cows graze, adjacent to the pattern of suburban row houses.

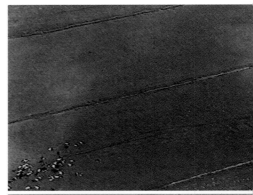

base

home fort
camp eml
cocoon coa
shelter wo
lap hole

ress place

brace nest

t cell shell

mb harth

den cave

Borneo Sporenburg
2500 Voids

Borneo/Sporenburg, Amsterdam
Design: 1993
Construction: 1996–2000
Size: 25 hectare, 2,500 housing units
Commissioner:
Project group Municipality
of Amsterdam

Borneo and Sporenburg are peninsulas in Amsterdam's Eastern Harbour Area, which new housing development will transform to new neighbourhoods. The assignment was to realise high-density, low-rise housing: one hundred units per hectare. The design is compelling and consistent; houses and streets alternate in a staccato rhythm. The ever-present water of the harbour offers sufficient counterbalance to the densely populated island, creating the intimacy and tension of the Dutch Water City.

Over twenty architects designed series of interlocking houses. In each house, fifty percent of the surface is devoted to introverted gardens or patios. Each house conceals a hidden world behind its facade.

By minimising public space, a maximum of individual outdoor space has been created. Private space is sharply divided from public space. There are no dubious semi-public zones, no obstacles and no front gardens. There are only houses or streets. Once out of the house, one is directly on his way.

At three strategic places this rhythm is interrupted by large apartment buildings. These sculptural blocks are beacons in the cityscape. They stand in relation to other high-rise structures in Amsterdam so that the peninsula islands are visually incorporated into the fabric of the city.

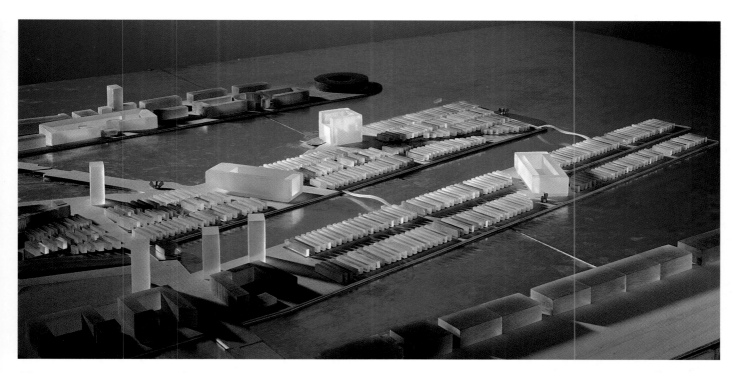

voids

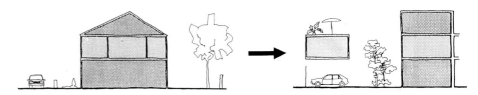

Outside space inside

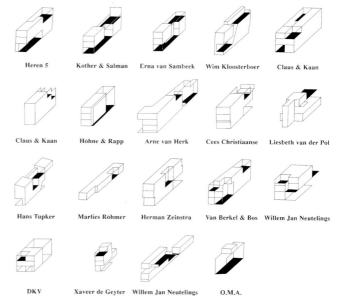

Heren 5   Kother & Salman   Erna van Sambeek   Wim Kloosterboer   Claus & Kaan

Claus & Kaan   Höhne & Rapp   Arne van Herk   Cees Christiaanse   Liesbeth van der Pol

Hans Tupker   Marlies Röhmer   Herman Zeinstra   Van Berkel & Bos   Willem Jan Neutelings

DKV   Xaveer de Geyter   Willem Jan Neutelings   O.M.A.

Architect:
Ruth Visser

Architect:
Neutelings Riedijk

voids

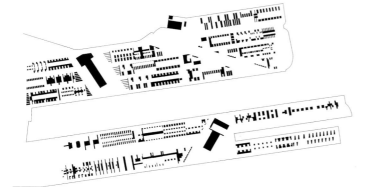

 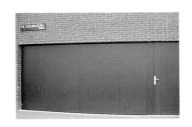 

 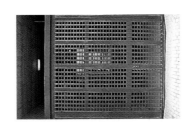 

 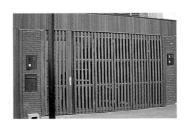 

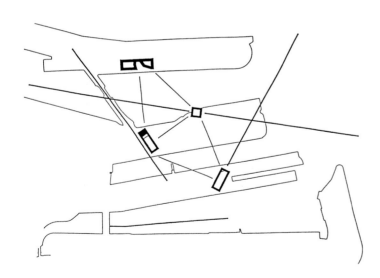

Intimate street.
Architect: Sambeek
& Van Veen

Ypenburg

Ypenburg, Den Haag
Design: 1998–2000
Realisation: 2000–2002
Houses: 639
Commissioner: D'Artagnan

Credits: Adriaan Geuze,
Edzo Bindels,
Jeroen de Willigen,
Amir Aman, Sybil Sträuli

The housing project Ypenburg is located in the polders around the city of The Hague. The mission was to design an urban plan for 700 new houses. To give individuality a chance in this suburban setting, and to avoid a monotonous character of the street facades, the design proposes to mix various housing types and to alternate the heights of the roofs. While the architecture of the houses is recognisably executed in the same style, the roofs make a rhythmical, lively counterpart.

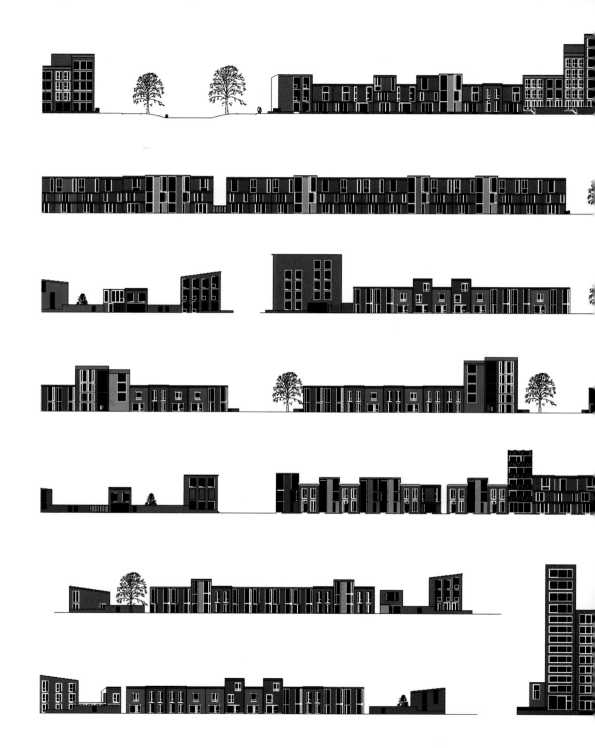

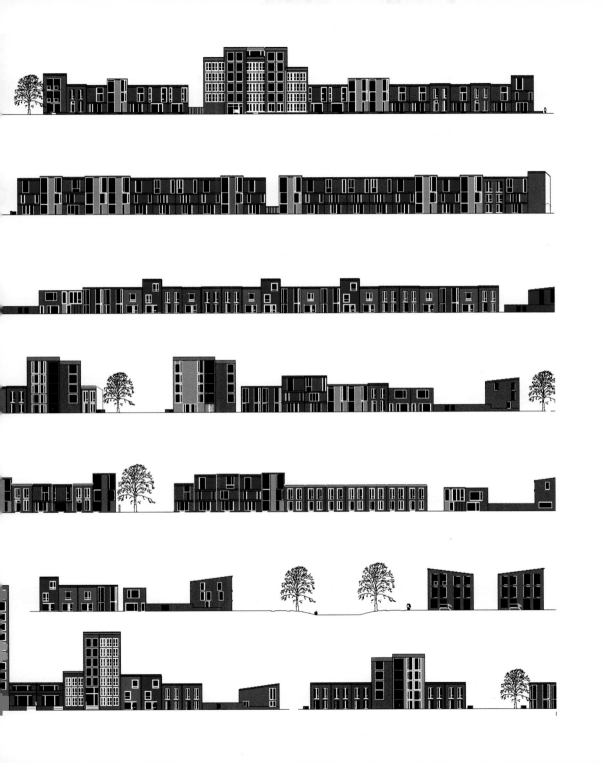

colonisation

colonise settle
appropriate
occupy invent
transform lay
invade set free
spoil cultivate
invent explore m

take claim
conquer found
clear expand
bare gain soil
identify flow
capture implant
anipulate inhabit

Buckthorn City

Buckthorn City, Hoek van Holland
Rotterdam 2045
Study design: 1995
Size: 4473 ha
Commissioner:
event steering committee
'50 years reconstruction -
50 years future'

The design of Buckthorn City is a study of the optimal sites for development in the region Rotterdam-The Hague. The scenario for the new city calls for reclaiming a portion of the sea, and is thus a clear departure from the steady development of the polder landscape. If a strip of land off the North Sea coast is reclaimed, it will be possible to allow the accelerated evolution of a landscape in five years.

Operation Duindoornstad will begin from two working islands in the sea. In the last phase of development, the northern island will be incorporated in a city. The second island will remain a monumental landmark off the new coast.

A 17-kilometre long dike of dunes will protect the new coastline and the inner area between the dike and the former coastline will be filled. The sand surface will be seeded with sea buckthorn (duindoorn) which will overgrow the area within two years. The former coast will be preserved, resulting in an elongated inner lake with run-offs and creeks. This rational work of engineering will be pitted against an unpredictable opponent. An 80-metre long, moving dune will be filled from the southern island. This unstable sand dune will fan out however chance may have it during the four to five years during which the new landscape will take form. Around this apocalyptic whim of nature, a city for 400,000 residents will develop.

Buckthorn

Swamp with Buckthorn
grid contours the City
Apocalypse of the dune

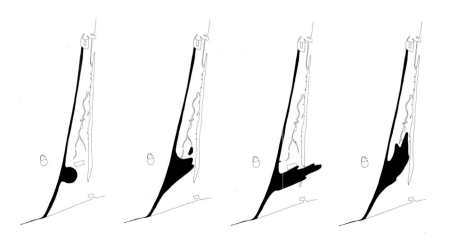

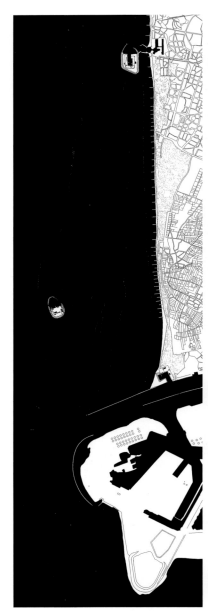

Before

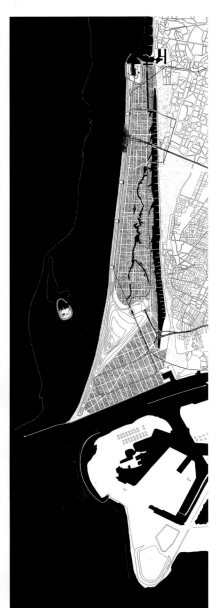

After

Highway to high rise city
Beach Boulevard
Creek City Centre

High rise city
Low rise housing area
Creek through villa village

Riem Park
Virgin city

Riem Park, Munich
Competition design: 1995
Size: 215 ha
Commissioner: MRG Maßnahmeträger
München-Riem GmbH

Munich parks

The English landscape style of eighteenth and nineteenth centuries resulted in a lasting polarity between the city and the city park. City and park have become opposites and are mutually exclusive. Yet from the viewpoint of urban evolution, the park can be considered the first phase of urban culture — green and vital, ready to absorb visitors and development.

The park design for the former airport Riem, near Munich, has been viewed as such. With an area of two hundred hectare, the park is in a league with prestigious parks like New York's Central Park. The ground plan for the new park is a city grid matching Manhattan in terms of density.

From a bird's eye view, the park looks like a city or an old fashioned garden with labyrinths and bosquettes. A closer view reveals that the park is divided into different compartments, each with its own sculptural quality. There is a block with hanging gardens, there are cubist and constructivist blocks and a Dali garden. Space has been set aside in the 'street pattern' for a recreational lake, playgrounds and exhibition spaces. It is an auto-free, green city, built up of elements from landscape architecture. Ambiguity governs the identity and the experience.

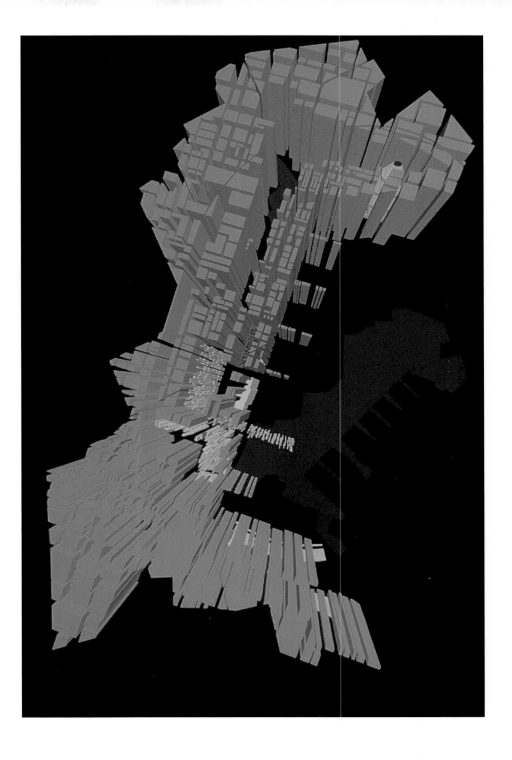

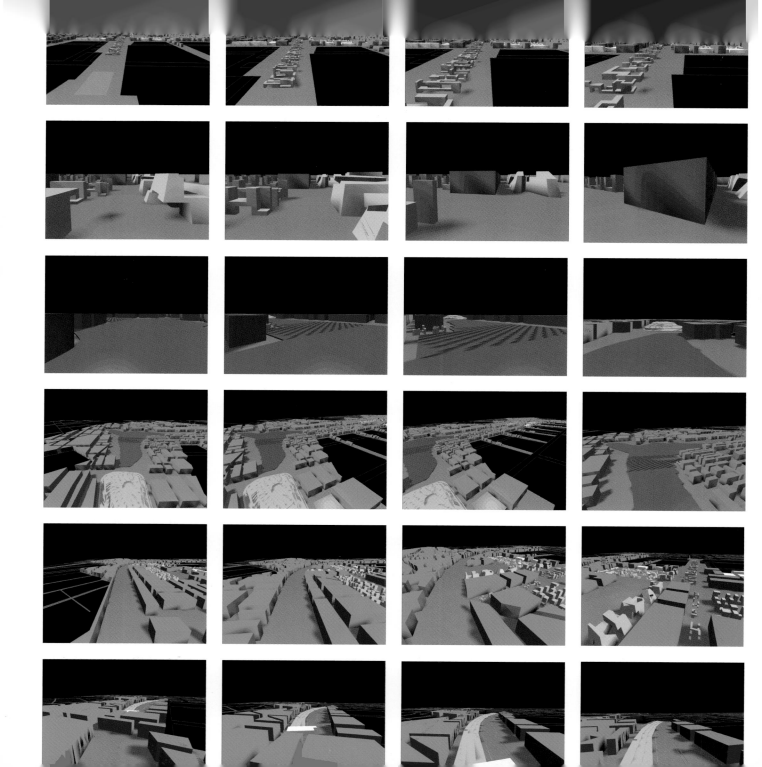

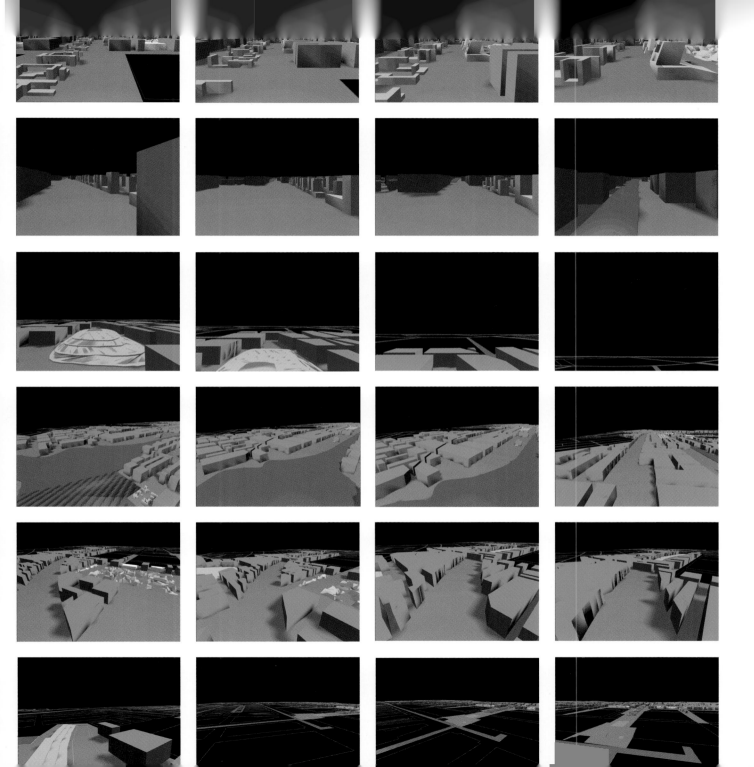

Zeeburg Island

Zeeburg Island, Amsterdam
Design (study): 1997,
in collaboration with Neutelings Riedijk
Size: 200 ha
Commissioner: City of Amsterdam
Housing units: 6,000

Directly on the ring road around Amsterdam, surrounded by water on all sides, lies the Zeeburgereiland. This is a wasteland with sewage cleaning plant and nomads from the city. The design explores the possibility of developing a city district with over 6,000 housing units with a direct relationship to the water — floating, on piers, on islands, on dikes and on pilings.

Construction begins by reclaiming the entire area with a grid of reed-lands. Viewed from the reed-lands, the infrastructure of the ring road takes on a heroic scale. The ecological reed-land is gradually colonised by city-dwellers. In addition to the areas between the reeds, two new water settlements can be inhabited.

Before

After

Vertical Landscape

Vertical Landscape, New York
Design study: 1996
Commissioner: West 8
StoreFront for Art and Architecture

Vertical Landscape is a manifesto to Manhattan's skyline and the tempestuous growth it projects on public and green spaces. Parks should be born of the same ambition that fired the Chrysler Building, the Empire State Building and Rockefeller Center. New York is the mother of all vertical cities — the ultimate city for the Babylonian garden.

The Manhattan grid organises the program of the city and offers architecture ultimate freedom. The architecture is vital, competitive and continually developing. The greenery is doomed to be a caricature of city greenery and is only permitted as filling for empty or leftover spaces. This causes it to remain a static factor, the result of routine conduct based on a cultural tradition. This contrasts with the restless nature of the city block. The green zones represent lifelessness where the city block represents life. The only sublime park is Central Park. This is a perfect emptiness covering 150 city blocks. The enclosed park provokes the skyline and sucks people into itself.

Accepting the grid as the life source reveals the unlimited potency of Manhattan. The Manhattan-principle of ambition and verticality is the basis for contemporary green interventions on Times Square, Columbus Circle, Madison Square and the setback of the Seagram Building on Park Avenue.

Time Square. Present situation

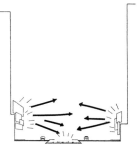

Time Square with vertical park

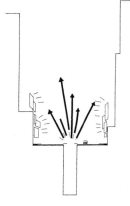

void

emptiness n
open still u
undetermin
blank vir
untouched
desire i

thing universe
occupied free
ed promise
gin clean
unstained
nvitation

ABN Amro Bank

ABN Amro Bank, Amsterdam
Architect: Willem Jan Neutelings,
Landscape architect: West 8
Competition design: 1992
Commissioner: ABN Amro Bank

The design for the ABN Amro Bank's new head office sky-scraper has an ingenious climate system. The air circulates behind the glass facade through large voids. The various activity divisions of the bank relate to these empty spaces. This 'Swiss cheese' design lends the structure its own identity even from the exterior when at night the differing sizes of the voids become visible through lighting.

The Mediterranean climate in the voids allows for creating subtropical planting. The design chosen for the interior gardens mimics, from bottom to top, the successive biotopes found on a Mediterranean mountain. Below are valley plants, in the middle are boulevard plants and at the top are plateau plants. Small, intimate patios are upholstered with shrubs and transformed into exotic gardens.

Climate control

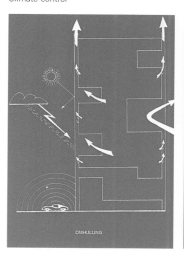

OMHULLING

Circulation

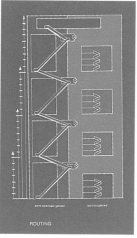

ROUTING

Gardens

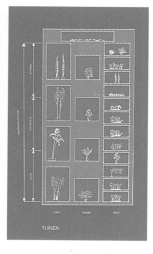

TUINEN

Theatre Square

Theatre Square, Rotterdam
Design: 1990–1992
Construction: 1996–1997
Size: 12,250 sqm
Commissioner: City of Rotterdam

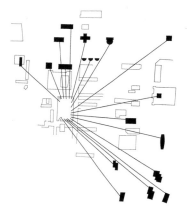

The Theatre Square is a podium from which Rotterdam's skyline is visible. The walking surface is 35 centimetres above ground level. No one can walk the square unnoticed; crossing the square is a conscious act. Once on the square, the visitor becomes an actor or spectator.

The square's floor is a mosaic of different textures. Wood, perforated steel plates, granite, epoxy and rubber elicit different activities. Football players, skeelers, children and musicians each choose their own zone. The square's surface is completely level. The only objects on the square are red light masts, the glass entrances to the underground parking garage and the 70-metre long city bench. On the eastern edge of the square stand three high ventilation towers, which together form a digital clock.

The four 35-metre high, hydraulic light masts echo the cranes in the harbour and serve as stage lights. These are spotlights in which lovers may capture each other and street singers may perform. The public may operate them so that a continuous mechanical ballet can be performed.

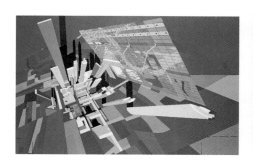

Anatomy
1. Cinema
2. Lightmasts and ventilation towers
3. Square surface
4. Structure
5. Roof
6. Parking

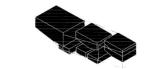

1

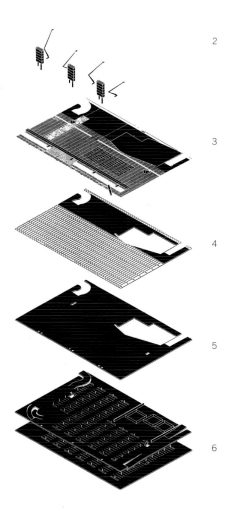

2

3

4

5

6

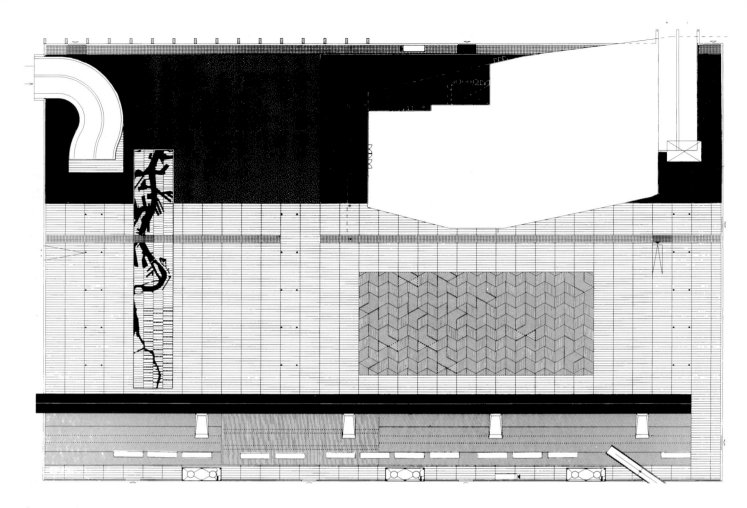

Square carpet

Wood

Epoxy

Steel

Kremlin

Kremlin/Leidsche Rijn, Utrecht
Competition design: 1997
Construction: 1999–2015
Size: complete park: 300 ha;
Kremlin: 70 ha
Commissioner: Municipality
of Vleuten de Meern

Can a 300-hectare city park exist within a vast late twentieth-century suburb? The question is whether a mono-functional, suburban culture is urbane enough to make an undeveloped area of this size a success. In the design for the Leidsche Rijn, part of the existing landscape is transformed to realise a park.

The edge of the park is cultivated to denote a transition from the sea of houses. This boundary simultaneously creates distance between the green area and the housing area. The park is an overtly empty space.

In total there are three concentric borders marking transitions between the different areas. The outermost edge is the 12-kilometre long, ecological and meadow-like Jacques P. Thijsse ribbon. This is a biking and hiking trail with views of the surrounding landscape. The water of the Leidsche Rijn forms the second landmark. Within this ring lies the core of the park — the Kremlin. This is a walled area of 50 hectare. This extremely introverted space is a paraphrase of Peking's Forbidden City, Tokyo's Emperor's Palace and Russia's Kremlin, but has the public function of a city park. Only a few entrances and a few waterways interrupt the 5-kilometre long wall enclosing the domain. Kremlin is a bounded, sacral space in which a characteristic environment will be created by a 'curator', who will arrange events and oversee the collection of gardens.

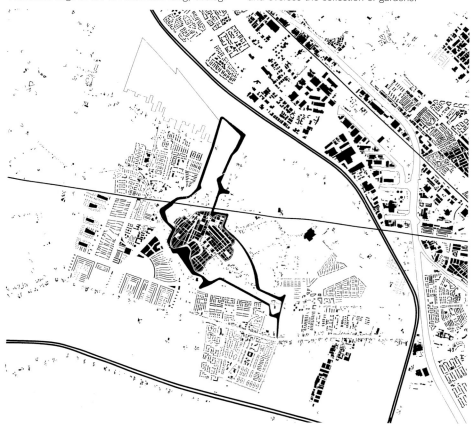

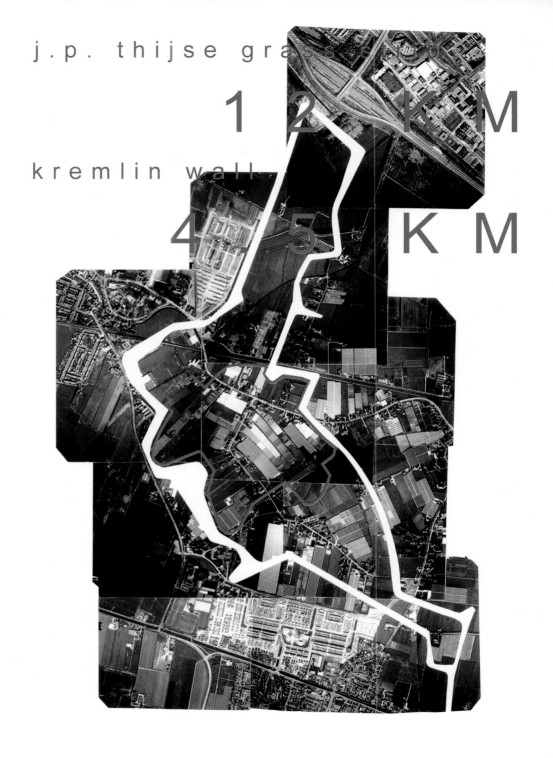

j.p. thijse gra...s...

1 2 KM

kremlin wall

4 5 KM

KREML

Cemetery San Michele

Cemetery San Michele, Venice
Competition design: 1998
Commissioner: City of Venice

Venice is like a dream that will be dreamt a million times by many people. The city evolves by reproducing itself and doing so, the city will become more and more perfect. The expansion of the cemetery San Michele raises several questions. What is the contemporary expression of a city for the deceased? What will be a recognisable emblem for Venice? And what will be the relationship between the old, existing island of the dead and the new, more efficient cemetery?

In the design is a series of dramatic themes.

The new cemetery is as rectangular as the existing one. An earth platform five metres above sea level holds a series of enclosed gardens with graves. Pedestrian circulation is possible within the system of colonnades, courtyards and patios. The design is also guided by the game of light and shadow. The colonnades filter a transcendental world. And the cemetery also opens vistas on to the lagoon. The design offers both a closed world for contemplating death and an opening to the world of the living.

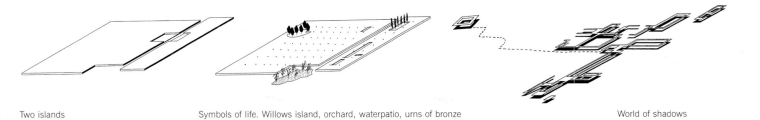

Two islands

Symbols of life. Willows island, orchard, waterpatio, urns of bronze

World of shadows

Cemetery in the lagoon.
Crematory patio split
in two by canal

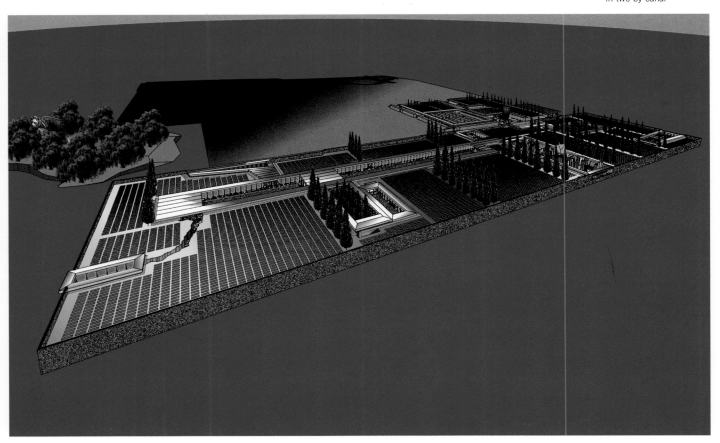

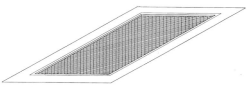
Stone patio

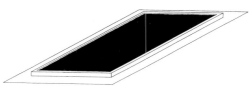
Water lily patio

Wells patio

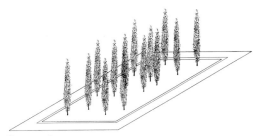
Cypresses patio

Chapel patio

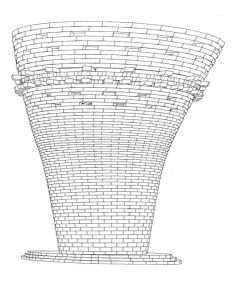

totem

magnet

nucleus oy

catalyst tur

event alier

momentu

point bo

seduction
ter springs
e dissonant
anecdote
m melting
mb solo

Leidsche Rijn Bridges

Papendorp Bridge
& Public Transportation Bridge
Design: 1998
Commissioner: Project office Leidsche Rijn

The City of Utrecht is planning two new bridges connecting the existing city to the western development Leidsche Rijn. The two bridges are a necessary link for bikes, trams and cars crossing the Amsterdam-Rijn Canal between old Utrecht and the future Leidsche Rijn district.

The Papendorp Bridge serves as a landmark in the landscape. Its large-scale lends mass and weight to the construction. The shape of the asymmetrical bridge changes continually in length as well as in cross-section. The land abutments have large areas without columns along the canal creating an open zone. The shore on the old city side is detailed to resemble a viaduct with steel columns in a slate surface.

The surroundings of the Public Transportation Bridge has a very pronounced structure; this prompted the choice for a sober design with a low profile on the site. The public transportation bridge rises from the point of an island in which the pylons are anchored with guys. The design of these pylons results from a power play: triangular where the guys grip, round near the ground and flat and bent at the top.

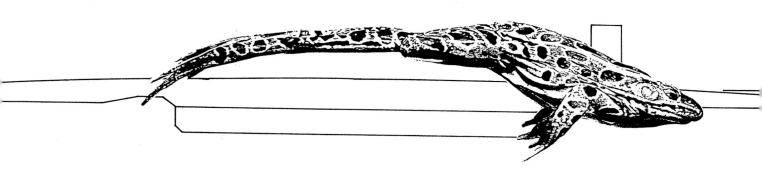

Papendorp bridge

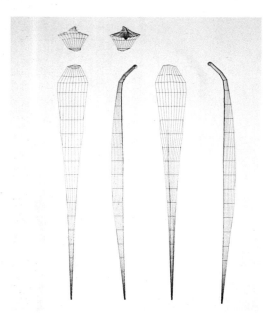

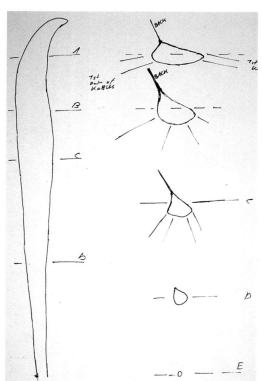

Borneo Sporenburg Bridges

Borneo Sporenburg Bridges
Design: 1998
Realisation: 1999–2000
Commissioner: Development
Company City of Amsterdam

The peninsulas Borneo and Sporenburg are connected by bridges. A double arched bridge in the east part and a low bridge in the west part span the 93-metre wide water channel over the railway basin at two points. These are transparent, steel trussed bridges with T-profiles and hardwood decks.

They crouch over the water like agile animals. A third bridge spans the 25-metre inner harbour and forms an essential link with the urban fabric. Built of 8-centimetre thick, solid granite plates, it alludes to the design of Amsterdam's classic bridges.

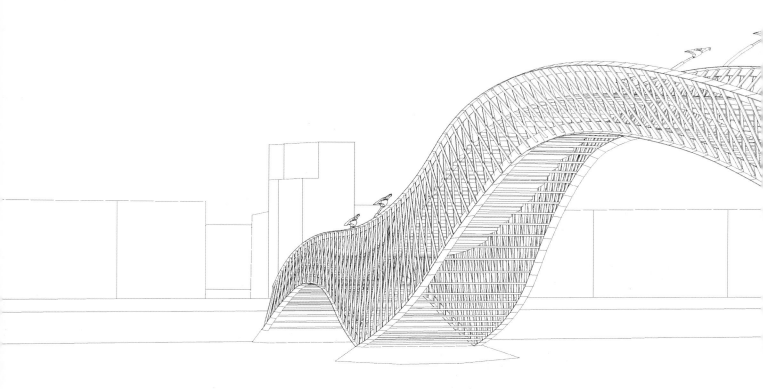

Study of transparent
structure

Study of dinosaur
shaped bridge

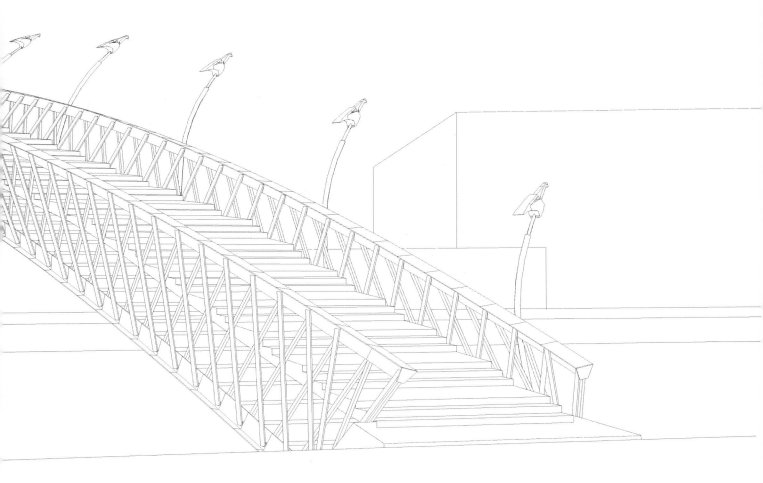

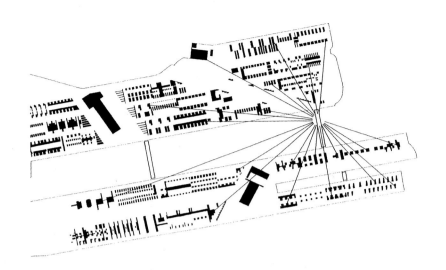

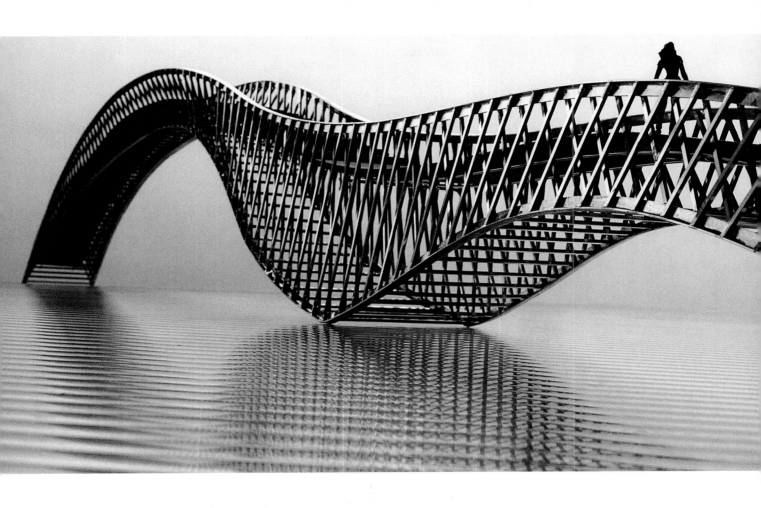

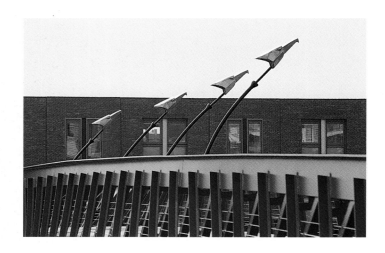

Elevated walkway

Elevated walkway, Emmen
Competition design: 1997
Construction: 1998–2000
Length: 300/550 m
Commissioner: Municipality of Emmen

In order to link the old and new zoo, a pedestrian traverse has been built right through the centre of Emmen. The covered path winds five metres above ground over the heads of shoppers and office workers. A series of alternating concrete feet support the path like upheld hands. There is contact with the outside world, the wind and the sun, yet the path rises above these realities. Four entrances are located at each end and two points along the route. The overhanging roof provides shelter. It is made of large slabs of slate overlaid in a scale pattern, fixed with steel pins into a steel net. The path dances through the city like a Chinese dragon.

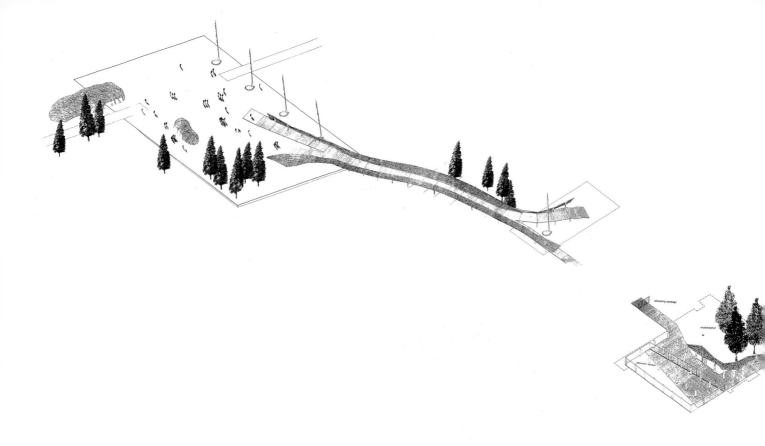

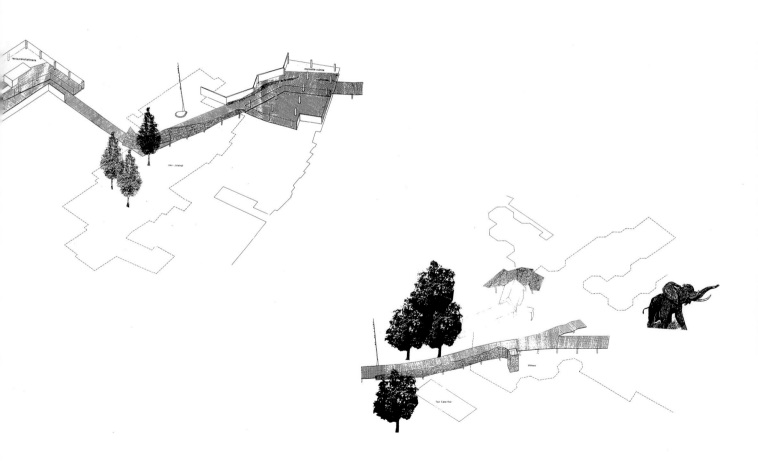

Carrasco Square

Carrasco Square, Amsterdam
Competition design: 1992
Construction: 1997–1998
Size: 45,000 sqm
Commissioner: City of Amsterdam

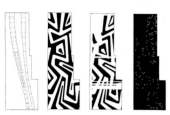

Anatomy:
railway tracks;
asphalt;
grass;
tree stumps

The Carrasco Square is part of Amsterdam's periphery. Offices, highways, tramlines and train rails are gradually overtaking the detached post of the city. The location is 'leftover' and lies hidden under the elevated rails. It is a passage for commuters who park their cars and board the train here and for rushed pedestrians who mow shortcuts through the grass on their way to the office. The space under the station has all the ingredients for eliciting anarchistic use. The assignment was to transform this wasteland into a park.

It was not possible to make a green oasis since the location lies for the most part in the shadow of the elevated rails. Ribbons of black asphalt, alternating with patches of grass, meander between the rows of columns. Where roads cross grass, the asphalt is patterned with white studs.

The graphic drawing defines the diffuse space and indicates the flow of traffic. The concrete columns are the trees of the city. Ivy will change them into thick green supports. A concrete cast of a beech tree has replaced one of the columns. Nature is immortalised in the mould of the artificial landscape. Spread over the grass stand long, hollow iron trees stumps with open lattices of tree rings. At night, light from the stumps illuminates the ceiling of rail lines, changing the space into a surrealistic fairy tale of light, sound and moving trains, endlessly reflected in the windows of abandoned office buildings.

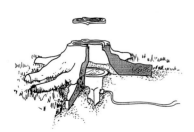

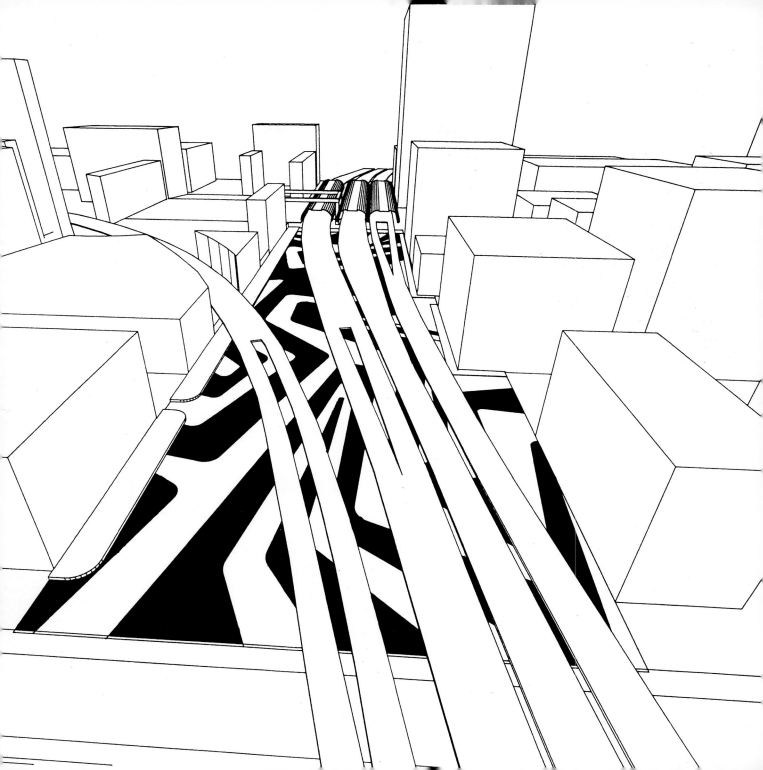

Aegon Square

Aegon Square, Den Haag
Competition design: 1996
Realisation: 2000–2001
Commissioner: Aegon NV

The square in front of the corporate building of insurance company Aegon will be transformed into a city garden. The base plan of the design reveals a typical urban morphology. The main eye catchers are the follies and a kiosk. These are covered with ivy, and some of them compete in height with the surrounding buildings. It is possible for various forms traffic to travel through the building-like structures. The concept for this city-garden is to create a reminder of nature in a strictly urban setting and not a surrogate nature, by means of a romantic park.

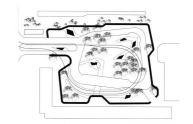

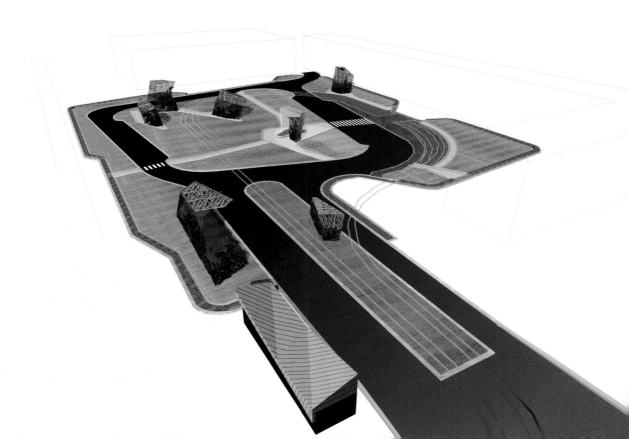

Expo-02
Landscape versus media

Expo-02 Yverdon
Design: 1999
Realisation: 2000–2002
Commissioner: Expo-02

Extasia: West 8, Diller & Scofidio,
Vehovar Jauslin, Morfing, Tech-Data

The Arteplage of Yverdon-les-Bains is one of the four sites at the Swiss lakes where the national exhibition takes place in 2001. A team of architects created a temporary landscape with explicit temptations of the senses. The public is invited to walk the paths that lead from the city of Yverdon-les-Bains to the shore of the lake. The paths meander through artificial dunes which are covered with extravagantly coloured flowers. The colours create psychedelic, dazzling patterns and the shape of the dunes bring the shapes of body parts to mind.

Two toned gravel pattern

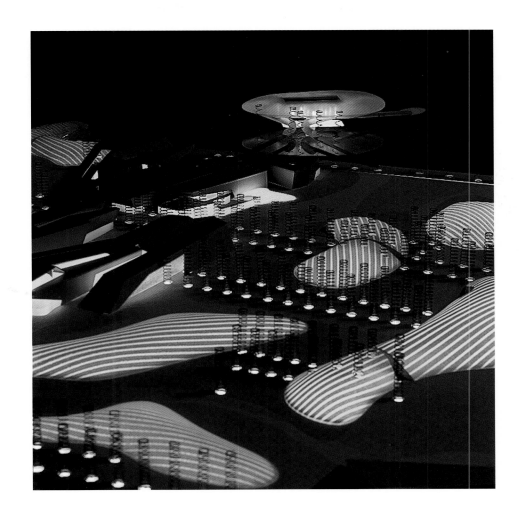

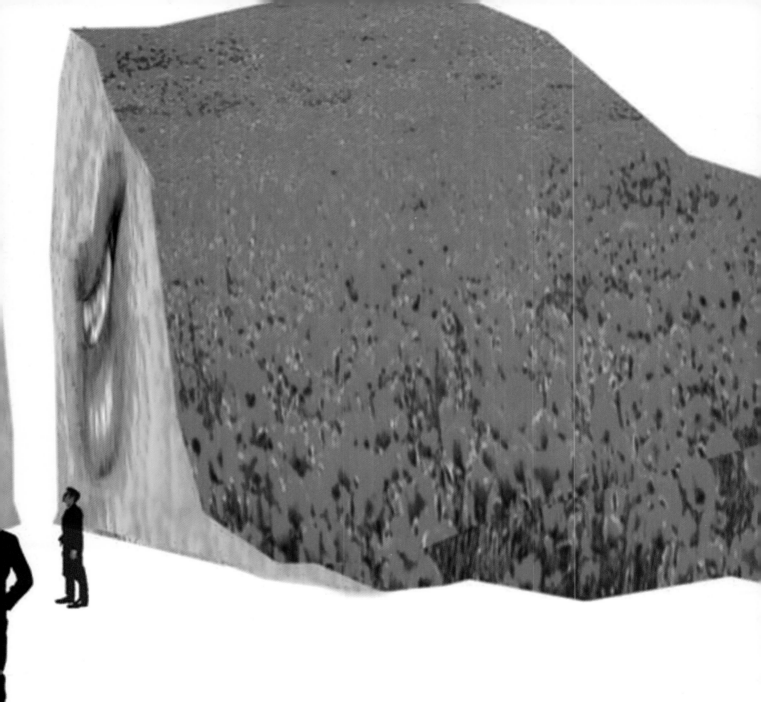

Mai - Juli 2001

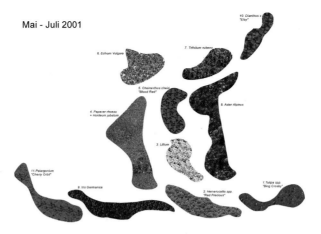

Juli - Augustus 2001

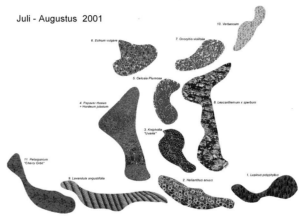

Augustus - October 2001

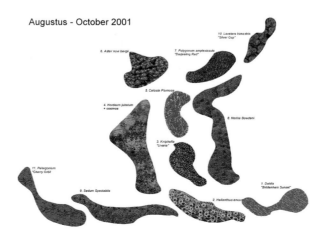

Following double page:
Media cut

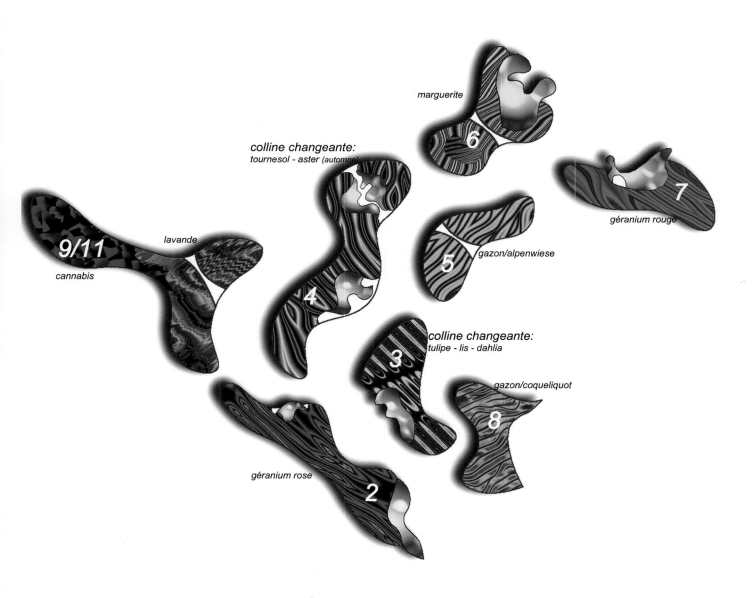

marguerite

6

colline changeante:
tournesol - aster (automne)

7

géranium rouge

9/11

lavande

cannabis

4

5

gazon/alpenwiese

colline changeante:
tulipe - lis - dahlia

3

gazon/coqueliquot

8

géranium rose

2

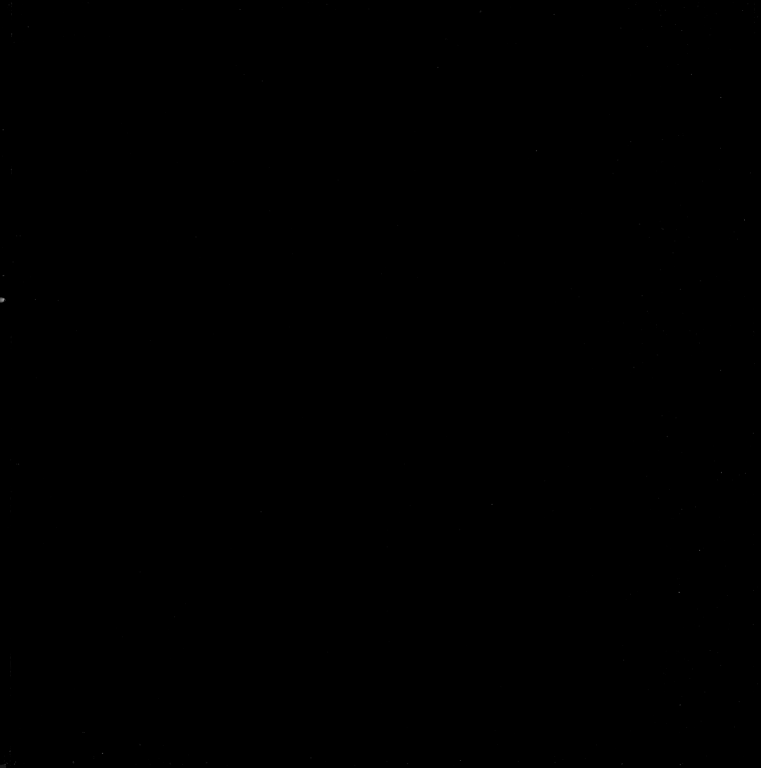

contemplation

feel wonde
sadness li
clarity
experie
memory si

r meditate
ght dream
imagine nce
nce zen
ence song

Secret Garden

Secret Garden, Malmö
Design: 1999
Commissioner: BoO1 City of Tomorrow

Situated on a landfill area the proposed garden dreams of the sea. It consists of an enclosed dark mikado forest cut into the shape of a cube with a side length of 12 metres. It is a mysterious garden to find your way through and to move in. Surrounded by a wall of logs of pine trunks it is an atmospheric interior mad of pine trunks with a maximum length of 17 metres. The ground is covered with blueberries. The wooden roof is painted falu-red and so are the vertical cuts of the trunks. When walking in the garden you discover a big shell belonging to another world. If you glance up you see the sky through three holes cut into a thick layer of seashells. Parts of huge rocks lying on the surface are visible. It is possible to climb up through the garden to this other lever by using ladders. Up here on the sea level the atmosphere is different and focuses on the nearby Öresund. The floor is covered with 60 centimetres of shells and several smooth rocks stick up to sit down and relax. Two big shells lie on the shell surface and collect water. The garden enables an imaginary relationship between the ocean and the Swedish forest.

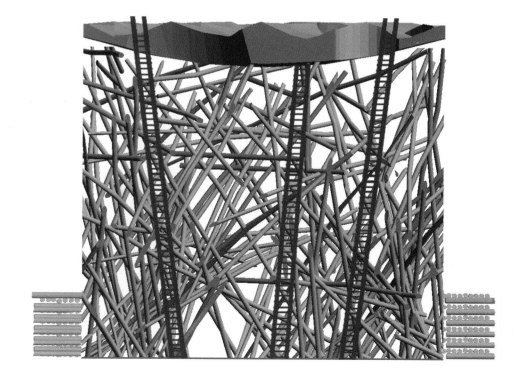

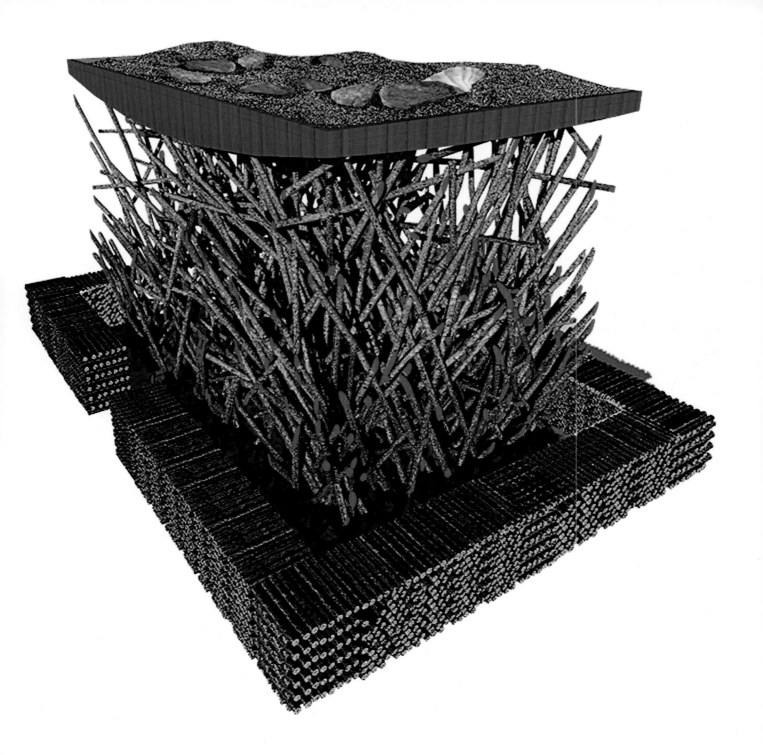

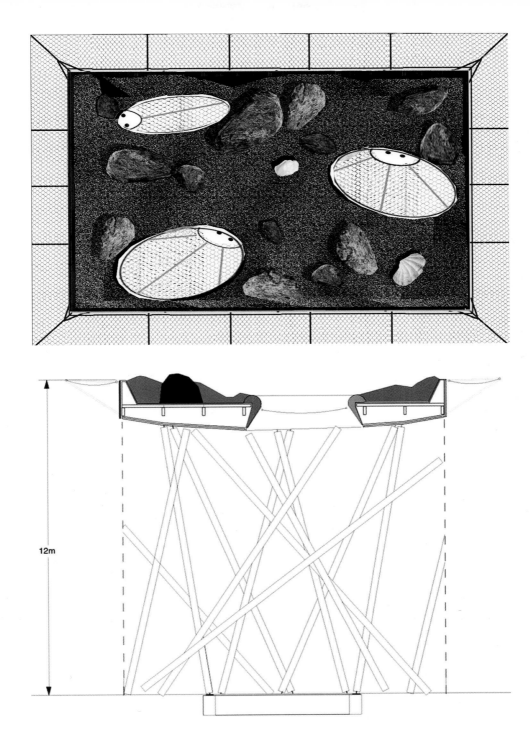

12m

Nymph Garden

Garden Makeblijde, St. Maartensdijk
Design: 1999
Construction: 2000
Commissioner: Makeblijde

At first a vertical landscape,
A tower of green, a golden blob

And then a romantic patio,
A contemplative inner sanctuary,
With lilies, frogs, a nymph.

Garden Makeblijde is a 7.5-acre park in which thirty gardens are situated. The gardens offer an insight into the design vision of contemporary landscape architects.

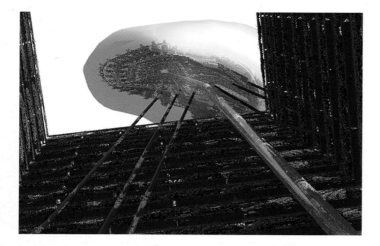

Cypresses Garden

Swamp Garden, Charleston
Design: 1997
Realisation: 1997
Commissioner: Spoleto Art Festival,
Charleston, USA

The mysterious swamp landscape around the city of Charleston evokes a fairytale-like beauty and at the same time it repels you. The silent water, high cypresses, the phallus-like sky-root tentacles of the cypresses and the deep croak of the frogs seem to have dictated the character of this landscape for ever. Nevertheless, these swamps are the leftovers of a man-made landscape.

In the times of slavery, these swamps used to be rice fields. When they were abandoned they evolved into swampy forest. The swamps are now home to alligators, frogs and turtles.

The silence and humid warmth compels people to meditate and merge with the landscape. A twisted boardwalk leads them from the solid grounds to an isolated open-air room amidst the cypresses. This secluded area is separated from the surrounding by layers of waving Spanish moss which is hung over wires. The ultra-light walls of moss move and change the light constantly, which results in an experience of surrealism through different atmospheres.

151

Project credits

One million houses
Adriaan Geuze,
Inge Breugem,
Jeroen Musch,
Guido Marsille,
Jeroen Jongeleen

Colonizing the void
Adriaan Geuze,
Edzo Bindels,
Jeroen Musch,
Jim Navarro,
Marc Lampe,
Ramon Jansen,
Aard Veldman,
David den Breejen,
Jack van Dyck

**Borneo Sporenburg -
2500 Voids**
Adriaan Geuze,
Wim Kloosterboer,
Yushi Uehara,
Sebastiaan Riquois

Buckthorn City
Adriaan Geuze,
Edzo Bindels,
René Marey,
Arno de Vries,
Guido Marsille,
Gricha Bourbouze,
Cyrus B. Clark,
Erik Overdiep,
Wim Kloosterboer,
Katrien Prak,
Ramon Jansen,
Suzanne van Remmen

Riem Park - Virgin City
Adriaan Geuze,
Edzo Bindels,
Fawad Kazi,
Guido Marsille,
Gricha Bourbouze,
David Buurma,
Wim Kloosterboer,
Hernando Arazola

Zeeburg Island
Adriaan Geuze,
Henk Hartzema,
Martin Biewenga,
Tom Cortoos

Vertical Landscape
Adriaan Geuze,
Edzo Bindels,
Jeroen de Willigen,
Jim Navarro,
Ramon Jansen,
Cyrus B. Clark,
Henry Borduin,

Marc McCarty,
Joost de Natris

ABN Amro bank
Adriaan Geuze,
Frans Parthesius

Theatre Square
Adriaan Geuze,
Wim Kloosterboer,
Dirry de Bruin,
Cyrus B. Clark,
Erwin Bot,
Dick Heydra,
Huub Juurlink,
Nigel Sampey,
Erik Overdiep,
Jürgen Beij,
Jerry van Eyck

Kremlin
Adriaan Geuze,
Edzo Bindels,
Jeroen de Willigen,
Rob Grotewal,
Bert Karel Deuten,
Martin Biewenga,
Suzanne van Remmen,
Nigel Sampey,
Joris Hekkenberg,
Jack van Dijk,
Esther Kruit,
Jacco Stuy,
Freek Boerwinkel,
Fritz Coetzee,
Maarten Buijs,
Edwin van der Hoeven

Cemetery San Michele
Adriaan Geuze,
Henk Hartzema,
Matteo Poli,
Cyrus B. Clark,
Martin Biewenga,
Oliver Krell,
Freek Boerwinkel,
Marnix Vink

Leidsche Rijn Bridges
Adriaan Geuze,
Daniel Jauslin,
Cyrus B. Clark

**Borneo Sporenburg
Bridges**
Adriaan Geuze,
Rudolph Eilander,
Maarten van de Voorde,
Daniel Jauslin,
Cyrus B. Clark

Elevated walkway
Adriaan Geuze,

Henk Hartzema,
Cyrus B. Clark,
Freek Boerwinkel,
Cees Verwey,
Marc Lampe,
Floor Moormann,
Maurice Käss,
Hiroki Matsura,
Olivier Scheffer

Carrasco Square
Adriaan Geuze,
Inge Breugem,
Dirry de Bruin,
Katrien Prak,
Olivier Scheffer,
Huub Juurlink,
Erwin Bot,
Jörn Schiemann,
Marnix Vink

Aegon Square
Adriaan Geuze,
Guido Marsille,
Cees Verwey,
Rudolph Eilander,
Sabine Müller,
Freek Boerwinkel,
Paul Deibel,
Edzo Bindels,
Edwin van der Hoeven

Expo-02
Adriaan Geuze,
Daniel Jauslin,
Jerry van Eyck,
Freek Boerwinkel,
Fritz Coetzee,
Rudolph Eilander,
Marco van der Pluym,
Maarten van de Voorde

Secret Garden
Adriaan Geuze,
Sabine Müller,
Lise Hellström

Nymph Garden
Adriaan Geuze,
Guido Marsille,
Sabine Müller

Cypresses Garden
Adriaan Geuze,
Cyrus B. Clark,
Marnix Vink,
Trevor Bullen